Ants Build

By Katie Berk

Scott Foresman
is an imprint of

PEARSON

Glenview, Illinois • Boston, Massachusetts • Chandler, Arizona • Upper Saddle River, New Jersey

Ants build.

Ants build with sand.

Ants build with sticks.

Ants build with leaves.

Ants build with pebbles.

6

Ants build tunnels.

Ants build nests.